As We See It

A SURVIVAL GUIDE FOR
COMMUNITY COLLEGE ADMINISTRATORS
AND TRUSTEES

As We See It

A SURVIVAL GUIDE FOR
COMMUNITY COLLEGE ADMINISTRATORS
AND TRUSTEES

ANDERSON | CRIST | NOVAK

As We See It

Copyright © 2009
John H. Anderson
Donald G. Crist
Charles R. Novak

Grateful appreciation is given to
Judi Anderson
for the cover concept and
formatting of this book.

*All rights reserved. No part of this book may be used or reproduced
in any manner whatsoever without written permission from the publisher,
except in the case of brief quotations embodied in articles and reviews.*

Published by

New Education Press*
6137 East Mescal Street
Scottsdale, Arizona 85254-5418

*An Imprint of Star Cloud Press
Scottsdale, Arizona

ISBN:
978-1-932842-37-1 — $ 12.95

Printed in the United States of America

We dedicate this book to
our nation's community colleges
and to their students.

In Way of Introducing Ourselves . . .

I had Cinch in a slow trot down a sandy wash that emptied into Blue Wash, the main stream bed that collects the run-off from the surrounding watershed. The Tonto National Forest was beautiful on this sunny morning; recent rains had made the desert landscape verdant with grasses and wildflowers. The sky was a brilliant blue, the temperature was a delightful sixty-five degrees, and all was right in this small, pristine part of the world.

As I approached the confluence with Blue Wash, I could feel Cinch anticipating whether we would turn right for a couple of hundred yards and head up Juniper Wash for an invigorating lope, or go left around the bend to where Camp Creek was gurgling along on the surface. But, then, he remembered that a well-trained horse doesn't participate in those decisions anyway. The sand in these mysterious washes is soft and deep, good for the horses' feet and excellent for their conditioning. Loping up these picturesque mini canyons takes one back a hundred years or more.

A light touch of the rein on Cinch's right neck signaled that we were going to the left where he would get a drink of cool fresh water. As we rounded the bend, a thicket of hackberry, desert broom and willows obscured our view ahead. We emerged from the thicket and then it happened—at that moment, and in that moment, several things occurred simultaneously. Cinch tensed, his head went up, his ears pointed and his nostrils flared. Alerted, I stopped the horse, raised in the saddle and looked where Cinch was looking. The stag stiffened, raised his head, and pointed his ears; water was dripping from his mouth and his nostrils flared. For a frozen moment in time we looked at each other; he was a magnificent creature with a wide six by six rack glistening in the sun. I wanted the moment to last, but it didn't. In the next instant the buck mule deer bolted and disappeared behind a jumble of boulders and mesquite. I waited a bit, trying not to let the image fade. Then I asked Cinch to walk upstream about a hundred feet to where a small pool had formed behind a pile of rocks. It was his favorite watering hole.

There I sat, mesmerized by the unspoiled beauty and the tranquility of this picturesque cowboy setting. How fortunate I was to be at this place, at this time, with my horse. I have come to prefer the company of a whole horse. Abruptly, my pleasant state of mind was interrupted by thoughts of my two deadbeat partners—what were they doing instead of working on our book? Don Crist was likely on the tennis court beating up on some 90-year-old gentleman with a bad leg. Later, he would insist that the guy was a level 5. Chuck Novak was no doubt pestering a smarter than he *salmo gairdnerri irideus* (a rainbow trout, if you are not an ichthyologist). I can visualize him up to his waist in one of the beautiful trout streams in Arkansas, working intently to tie just the right fly on the end of his tippet. The fish, bored, had slipped upstream: virtuoso performances.

The three of us became acquainted while serving as community college presidents in Illinois . . . Chuck at Richland, Don at Carl Sandburg, and I at Black Hawk and Rock Valley. I explained that Interim Presidents only serve about a year. They said I couldn't hold a job. We enjoyed getting together at meetings and conferences to share experiences, i.e., embrace challenges and find solutions. As much as we were alike professionally, our personalities were quite different . . . an intriguing mix. We shared a passion for the mission of the community college, we wanted our students to succeed, and we demanded more money from the state, etc. Serving as a community college president has to be one of the most exciting and fulfilling jobs there is, and we loved it. Eventually one of us asked the question, "What shall we do after?" Well, just sitting on the porch wouldn't suffice. We still had spirit and energy and a desire to contribute. And, yes, we felt we had something to offer from our seasoned experience. We decided to form a consultancy, called SYNERGY STRATEGISTS, dedicated to helping community colleges when they had special challenges or needs. In this work, we often wished that some former community college presidents had written an easy-to-read guidebook, wherein they had discussed what it is like to serve as a community college president, as well as the problems that one faces, the philosophies that endure, the solutions that work, the land mines to avoid, etc. Finally, we pondered whether or not we should write such a book.

And we did, and now we offer it to you. We hope it will provide real and practical assistance to those brave souls who are doing their best in administrative positions or who are serving as trustees in our nation's community colleges. Never underestimate the importance of these high callings, or of the privilege of serving in these capacities.

Books about administration and leadership in America's community colleges are plentiful. The great majority of these publications are carefully researched, skillfully written, and contain a wealth of valuable information.

This offering takes a somewhat different approach. First, it is meant to provide some humor. Second, it is not based upon empirical data or meticulous research; rather, it is based upon experience and practical application. The three authors are career professionals in the community college and have extensive service as college presidents. This book is an effort to share the lessons learned from that service. It is not a story so much as it is a collection of thoughts and anecdotes. Although we endeavored to give it a logical pattern, it does not flow like a novel. Nevertheless, it is our hope that it will serve as a survival guide for those who aspire to become, and for those who desire to remain, community college presidents or college trustees.

Finally, this book is written in aphoristic style—simple, short statements which cast a clear thought into the stream of consciousness. It is the authors' hope that these aphorisms will be easier to recall and easier to find if rereading is required. Most of the aphorisms are followed by a short explanation; some are followed by longer explanations; others need no explanation. They are, we hope, golden nuggets that we mined from our years of service in the noble enterprise.

—JOHN H. ANDERSON

Foreword

The American Community College movement has become an international movement. Why would other nations want to replicate this movement, this institution of higher education? The answer can be simple or complex depending upon your perspective, but the foundation is the same . . . people helping people to develop personally and professionally.

The American public has learned throughout history that the success of our organizations, both public and private, is truly dependent upon the people comprising them. Now, enter the global environment where boundaries have been erased, or at least blurred, and the continued success of our organizations will, again, depend upon the people doing the work to compete in this new, expanded arena. And, it will be the community college that, again, acts to develop in our citizens new personal and employment skills, as well as the preparation to excel in universities at home and abroad. Additionally, the community college must continue to strengthen its evolving role in economic development as well as its expanding partnership with the nation's K-12 system.

This is a comprehensive and ambitious mission, but it is also the reason that the American Community College is an essential ingredient to this country's success, and it is why other countries want to emulate the American system. Thus, we need visionary leaders in our community colleges. It is the passion of past and current leaders that has defined our success to this point, and it will be your passion that defines a future that no other sector of higher education shall match.

In the spirit of the community college approach to personal and professional development, we bring the teachings and advice of our experts to you. The three authors of this book are such experts. I am personally and professionally acquainted with each of them and the wisdom they have shared is fundamental to success in an education system that has become a world leader on many fronts. The lessons they have learned in their careers are illustrated for you as a guide, a primer, for your community college administrative career. Take to heart their teachings and use their book as a reference as you progress in your own career and carry the "people's college" to new heights.

KEITH MILLER, Ph.D.
President, Greenville Technical College
Chairman of the Board, American Association of Community Colleges

Preface

The community college is a truly American invention. It was invented, with necessity as its mother, on a fundamental premise—to democratize higher education. It worked! With passion as its driving force, and access as its hallmark, millions of ordinary Americans soon found higher education easily available to them. Our society was elevated, as the junior/community college became the "melting pot" for post high school education and preparation for career entry or for university transfer. The junior college evolved into the community college and, unlike the universities, developed a genuinely comprehensive and unique mission: to become their community's multiple resource center.

While community colleges cannot be all things to all people, they do provide higher education services for all who can and will. And they do so to the limit of their resources and to the extent of their vision and creativity. The community college provides the opportunity for people to move from the bleachers to the box seats. In the early days of the community college movement, there was reticence by some people to accept the quality these new colleges provided and reluctance by universities to accept their credits for transfer. Now, one hundred years later, the community college movement has matured. We believe that our nation now understands and supports the community college and its comprehensive mission. They are well past the era of uncertainty, having earned their stripes and solidified their proud identity. The community college will continue to enjoy the confidence of the nation as long as it remains close to its customers and the communities it serves.

All presidents have stories to tell that illustrate the impact of their colleges on the lives of their students, on the communities, and, indeed, on their own lives as well. In fact, they talk enthusiastically about the importance of the community college to the nation, and of the responsibility it has to reflect the community it serves. This is how presidents and boards formulate the vision and implement the mission of their colleges. Community college presidents rightly consider themselves privileged to serve "the people's college."

As former community college presidents, the authors are pleased to share their musings and their observations with those who carry on the work of the nation's community colleges. It is the goal of this book to provide information and inspiration for administrators, trustees and state board members that might assist them in pursuit of their college's high expectations. In the end, the experience and wisdom of these seasoned leaders in higher education should offer some insight and delight for any college administrator and trustee.

Here is a simple guide book for use in the diagnosis and treatment of the condition known as "college president." It is a malady both chronic and intoxicating with which one is either afflicted or not. Some of what has been written may act as an analgesic balm to soothe the symptoms. This, and small doses of individual student success, will provide welcome relief; be glad of it, for there is no antidote.

It is important to note that the opinions of John Anderson, Donald Crist, and Charles Novak in this survival guide, are just that—their opinions. They are based on experience from their career work in the community college, and these presidents sometimes offer different approaches to the same issue. Such diversity actually mirrors what happens in a real work setting.

TABLE OF CONTENTS

IN WAY OF INTRODUCING OURSELVES	i
FOREWORD	v
PREFACE	vii
CHAPTER ONE	
So, You Want To Be A Community College President?	1
CHAPTER TWO	
Good Leadership: Values and Ethics	5
CHAPTER THREE	
Good Leadership: Vision	9
CHAPTER FOUR	
Good Leadership: Practice	13
CHAPTER FIVE	
Employee Relations	25
CHAPTER SIX	
The External President: Politics and Relationships	31
CHAPTER SEVEN	
The Workings of the Board of Trustees	39
CHAPTER EIGHT	
Who Will Lead: Shades of the Almighty	49
CHAPTER NINE	
Other Musings and Observations	55
CLOSING THOUGHTS	63
About the Authors	69-71
Consultation Services Information	73

Chapter One

"If you need applause, try show business."—Anonymous

SO, YOU WANT TO BE A COMMUNITY COLLEGE PRESIDENT?

There is an old saying that suggests the "grass always looks greener on the other side of the fence." Holding that thought often causes a yearning to travel to the other side, only then to discover that the water bill there is considerably higher.

Some college administrators set a professional goal of becoming a college president. The American Association of Community Colleges, the League for Innovation and the Association of Community College Trustees have conducted leadership programs designed to prepare administrators for community college presidencies, and a good number of the participants in these programs have become presidents.

Having served in such positions long enough to have a good feel for it, some presidents have quipped to each other, or to themselves, "Why did I want this job?" Though you will not often hear it said, the president's role is revered, as it should be. The reality is, it is not easy to be an effective president. Although, some may admire the president when things go well, most do not envy or seek the position. While many college employees feel qualified and entitled to criticize the president, few actually want to be president. Hopefully, there will continue to be some deans and vice presidents sufficiently courageous to desire the position. If you believe you can, you can. That is a fundamental ingredient in effective leadership. Be assured, that as president, you will have the opportunity to lead and to accomplish great things. The role is both a genuine privilege and a demanding responsibility. The authors appreciate and respect our fellow presidents, and we congratulate those who have decided to become a college president. You are needed.

We hope the reader will take advantage of our good, and not so good, experiences and garner from them a clearer assessment of whether they would be effective in such a role. The presidency is, and will always be, a very important position, and those who choose this path will encounter much of what is discussed in the pages that follow. The authors have developed this chapter to give aspiring administrators a glimpse of the challenges of the position prior to the actual experience. For those who are already college presidents, perhaps there will be some shared recognition and humor in these anecdotes.

John Anderson...

If You Have No Interests in Life Other Than Work, You Could Be a College President

If You Are the Kind of Person Who Wakes Up in the Morning and Looks Forward to Ridicule and Contempt, You Could Be a College President

If You Enjoy Working 70 Hours per Week for Near Volunteer Wages, You Could Be a College President

If You Need to Be Reminded On a Daily Basis That You Are Incompetent, You Could Be a College President

If You Like Having Ten Things to Do, and Time for Five, You Could Be a College President

If You Believe You Can Squeeze a Diamond Out of a Lump of Coal, You Could Be a College President

If You Think Board Meetings Are Fun, You Could Be a College President

If You Find It Stimulating to Sit on a Committee That Requires Ten Months to Draw a Ten Minute Conclusion, You Could Be a College President

Chuck Novak...

If You Can Walk Through a Picket Line and Convince Yourself That the Participants Are Behaving Professionally, You Could Be a College President

If You Can Continue to Work Diligently on a Plan for the College's Future Amid Accusations of Lack of Leadership and Communication, You Could Be a College President
HOWEVER . . . on a more positive note . . .

John Anderson...

If Hearing the Strains of *Pomp and Circumstance* Captures Your Soul, You Could Be a College President

If You Are Inspired by the Energy That Pervades the Campus at the Beginning of Fall Semester, You Could Be a College President

If You Anticipate Commencement Exercises With Joy, You Could Be a College President

If a Late Friday Afternoon Smile and Hello from a Passing Student Transforms a Bad Week into a Good Week, You Could Be a College President

If You Are More a Sower than a Reaper, You Could Be a College President

If You Solidly Believe That Education Elevates Humanity, You Should Be a College President

Chapter Two

GOOD LEADERSHIP: VALUES, ETHICS AND MORAL AWARENESS

The aphorisms in Chapters 2, 3 and 4 are about "good leadership." Chapter 2 explores the necessity for moral awareness in an organization. Chapter 3 explores the elements of a vision—everyone seeing where they are going. Chapter 4 explores the concept of good leadership—its traits, its ways, its outcomes.

Chuck Novak…

To Create a Value Driven Organization, the Organization's House Must Be in Order

Creating a value driven organization requires moving the entire enterprise to a higher level of consciousness and sustaining it. If employees do not understand the basic expectations of the workplace; if there is job insecurity, or other nagging labor issues, the organization is not ready. Four conditions must be in place before moving toward a value-driven enterprise: (a) financial stability and security, (b) a clear purpose and mission, broadly understood, (c) clear public policies which establish expectations, and (d) a genuine desire at all levels to involve employees in the life of the organization.

Mission Gives an Organization Purpose, Values Give It a Heart

There are different kinds of values. In the case of a values driven organization, moral values are the kind that gives organization its character, its personality and its heart. Today's need for moral awareness is being constantly driven by new technology which leverages behavior and decisions. Discussing values in the work place engages the organization in studying the consequences of its decisions and work activity.

Values Define the Manner in Which We Will Work; Not What We Do, But How We Do It

Workplace discussions about individual and organizational values will create a new relationship between the employer and the employee. Such discussions do not detract from understanding and knowing the purpose of work. Instead, such discussions bring to work a new focus, a focus on how employees achieve the outcomes of work with each other.

Values Are the Quality of Our Character

Values guide behavior. If a person embraces the moral value "respect," then the person will manifest behaviors which demonstrate respect for property, for actions, and for people. Values will guide our treatment of others; they guide our hope for others; they guide our service to others.

Values Are First an Individual Expression, Then a Group Expression, and Ultimately, an Organizational Expression

Organizations manifest certain kinds of behaviors only because the individuals in the organization prefer certain sets of values which cause the behavior to be manifest. When an organization manifests a set of values as it carries out its work, it does so because the people in the organization have a learned, common value set that gives the organization the direction and strength needed to express the values set as an organizational culture.

An Organizational Value Set Does Not Just Happen, It is Inspired and It is Learned

Group behavior is driven by the people who make up the group. If everyone in the group acts in a consistent manner, they do so because they have taught each other the worth of that type of behavior. Values guide behavior. Behavior is an individual expression before it is a group expression. Group behavior is driven by learned, common preferences of the individuals in the group. A values driven organization is built from the bottom up to the top.

Values Are the Apex of the Organizational Hierarchy

Values are at the top of the organizational hierarchy; they affect everything because they are the how. They go to the manner and nature of work—how we work with each other and students. Mission and purpose are the what; they point direction. Organizational goals are next followed by objectives and activities which will achieve these goals. Put these elements together and they become an institutional plan created under a set of overarching principles called values.

Becoming a Leader Is a Journey Inward

Good Leadership hunts for your soul. It wants to know who you are, and what you will do. How will you make a better place to live and work? It digs into your core; you take the journey. You fail; you triumph. You fall to the ground; and you stand up. You stand, you speak, you lead, and you go on. They will either follow or they won't. It depends on you.

Chapter Three

GOOD LEADERSHIP: VISION

John Anderson...

Your College Will Have a Future Whether You Plan For It or Not

If you plan for it, it will reflect your vision; you will be the composer and not a musician playing someone else's tune.

Don Christ . . .

If the Focus of the President Is the Glass Is Half Empty, the President Will Become a Glass Half Empty

Often the contrarians of an organization are the ones who gain the attention of the president. They are the squeaky wheels; they are the glass half empty people who bring forward or create problems, but never solutions; they are the ones who represent the weakest link in the chain. Unfortunately, more often than not, those who listen to them are pulled down to their level and become like them. It rarely ever works the other way. These people seem to choose to be unhappy, and want to share their unhappiness with their colleagues and students. They are present in all organizations, they seldom change their stripes, and they will drag the president down if given the attention they do not deserve.

At times presidents attempt to help these unhappy individuals, and recognize they have talent and expertise that, if channeled in the right direction, can contribute much to the college. Unfortunately, the time and energy required for this is more than the college's champions and students can afford to have the president give.

Surround Yourself with People Who Are Better Than You

Some presidents look to the success of their vice presidents to determine their own effectiveness as a president. This, of course, isn't the only indication of a president's leadership performance. It is a sound practice to surround yourself with people who are better than you in their areas of responsibility. This enables the president to spend time developing and articulating the vision and mission for the college. Otherwise, the president gets bogged down in putting out fires and managing processes. The board expects the president to be the president, and leave vice presidential responsibilities to the vice presidents. Good and talented people who surround the president will make this possible.

The President Is the Champion for Accreditation at All Levels within the Organization and Throughout the College District Because It Is That Important

Accreditation is critical to the credibility of all colleges, to the continuance of many vocational programs, and to transferability of academic credits. The planning and organization required for accreditation on-site visits is time consuming and can be problematic for some presidents. This is not a time to distance one's self from the process or underestimate the impact and value of the outcomes. The best course is for the president to involve himself in the development of the institutional self-study, support the efforts of the evaluation team and be responsive to the findings and recommendations that are institutional or program specific.

Chuck Novak...

A Vision Has Substance and Endures

A vision exists for a reason, and becomes reality through change. A vision is a conception, an idea, a way of becoming, of building. It is not so abstract that it cannot be done. A vision is not a dream; it is a dream coming true. It is observable behavior and has substance. People are mortal and a vision may be immortal: A vision becomes a way of thinking, behaving and achieving — a way of living. Visions live, change and adapt beyond the leaders who first articulated them.

A Vision Can Be Simply Stated

Although working toward a vision may be a complex and multi-faceted effort, the notion or description of the vision is best expressed in a plain, short statement. One college said it this way: "People helping people build a better community."

A Vision Needs People to Embrace It

A vision begins to materialize when people adopt its tenets and begin teaching it in an articulate and persuasive manner. Leaders who inspire vision are not always what people typically think they should be. They teach rather than direct; they persuade rather than coerce; they encourage rather than compel; they serve rather than demand. They lead through persuasion, not coercion, and through articulate presentation of their vision so that it contributes to the quality of life and living. The people who follow choose to follow, and they embrace the vision by taking it beyond the person who taught it.

Leadership Which Inspires Vision and Benefits Society Is Founded in and Around a Moral Core

Good leaders bring to their work certain values, beliefs, understandings and viewpoints—the moral core. The moral core contains moral values which guide behavior and relationships. It contains work values which inspire achievement and accomplishment. It contains a sense of the future and of what can be, which inspires vision. Leaders who have not totally evolved a moral core tend to respond to events and pressures. Leaders who have developed the core create events and dissipate the pressures. A college president has a set of principles along with a set of duties.

Chapter Four

GOOD LEADERSHIP: PRACTICE

John Anderson...

Leadership Is the Artful Science of Facilitating Problem-Solving and Otherwise Meeting the Needs of Group Members So That They Are Free to Enjoy the Pursuit of Their Common or Individual Goals

An effective leader is like the brush guard on a locomotive. They both remove the obstacles to assure clear passage. Group members are more creative, effective and happy when the path is clear and they know the destination.

Leaders Lead People, Manage Process, and Supervise Performance

People do not like to be managed; they will, however, agree to be led if they have confidence in the leader. So, lead people and leave the managing for processes. Likewise, you should direct supervision more toward the employee's performance and less toward the employee.

When Something Goes Right, the President Gives Credit to Others; When Something Goes Wrong, the President Accepts the Responsibility

I don't know how it got to be that way, but that's the way it is. Following this rule will bring respect and allegiance—albeit, never in generous portions.

Imperfection Is the Catalyst for Progress

It follows, then, that imperfection is a natural ingredient in the scheme of things—an illuminator. Embrace it, but gingerly.

The President Must Always Be Super-Hero!

The president cannot be sick, unhappy, discouraged, angry, uninformed or without a plan—ever! It may not be fair, but it is expected.

Change Is Not an Occasional Clash of Cymbals; It Is the Melody

A few people embrace change as an exciting part of their lives; some people are indifferent to change; the majority of people, it seems, are terrified by change and reactively oppose it. When it is presented singularly and with a bang, many people are frightened by it. When it is seen as a continually evolving part of the college's strategic plan, and is implemented incrementally, it can be less terrifying. Make it a hum rather than a crescendo. But, there may be times when a bang is unavoidable.

The Leader Is a Generalist, the Generalist Is a Leader: They Are One

Most people begin their work life in a job which requires a specialized skill set. It makes no difference in what sector they work—government, education, business, industry or the various professions. Some will engage the specialist skill set their entire career; others will take a journey on the road to leadership. Their beginning skill set is placed on a shelf, and they begin to learn a new one. They begin to learn the art of seeing as a generalist, greeting broader ranges of thought and consideration which test the effect of their actions on everything. The leader/generalist must, of necessity, have an objective, unobstructed, and three dimensional view of any issue. Only then can he represent the plethora of interests impacting an issue.

A Good Leader Is At the Front of the Pack, Not in Front of the Pack

If you are "in front of" the pack, you don't know if you are being followed or chased. At the front you are one of the pack and a participant in what is being discussed and proposed; you are in a position to "know what is going on." And, you can be more helpful to your group.

Some Presidents Have More Style than Substance; Others Have More Substance than Style

In the short run, style sometimes prevails. In the long run, effective presidents develop a generous portion of each. Both are important like wrapping and content. A nicely wrapped package will attract attention and encourage a look at the contents—be prepared not to disappoint. You accumulate substance through credentials, experience and seasoning; you develop style through training and practice.

The President Must Always Do the Right Thing. If You Get Criticized For It, Do It Anyway

The right thing to do is usually clear to everyone. However, there will be those who oppose it for reasons of self-interest. It falls to the president to gain a consensus, whenever possible, but to take the right action in any case. Be cautioned not to mix implementation process with the merit of the issue. Leadership is doing the right thing; management is doing the thing right.

Though Sweet, No Doubt, Yours Is Not the Only Tune to Be Heard

When the president asked his astute assistant, Nancy Chamberlain, "What am I supposed to do at this meeting?" She replied, "Sit in the back and be quiet." GOOD ADVICE! Allow others to speak; do not feel that you must interject every time something is said; use restraint even when you know something being said is inaccurate; try to wait until you are asked to respond; refrain from unnecessary rhetoric; develop your skill for patience and your tolerance for silence. Of course, you know what the outcome or conclusion must be, but allow them, or help them, arrive there at their pace. This is a time when the process is very important. Listen.

It Is At Least Amusing How Maturity Reveals the Brilliance of Gray

Democracy is agonizingly inefficient, but astonishingly effective. Therefore, the president's toolbox must include an oversized instrument for compromise. Early in my youth, at fifty, it seemed everything should be black or white and, if necessary, forced it to be so. After becoming a college president, there have been only shades of those two colors, and an appreciation for gray has emerged.

Leadership Requires Courage

In the exercise of courage, a president must respect the process, but champion the outcome. You will often find yourself walking into the wind—sometimes alone. Effective leaders take risks, and this takes courage because it is difficult to be on target every time. When you're not, it takes courage to acknowledge the fact, take the heat, and try again. Do not lose sight of the end.

Being a Leader Does Not Make You a Leader

Having the title or holding the position does not make you effective in the role. Without the necessary skills and abilities, you will be a leader in name only. However, if you find yourself in the position and you have the potential, and your followers will give you the time for on-the-job-training, you might become a leader. It is not something that automatically comes with the title, so do as much as you can to get ready ahead of time.

Accomplishment Is Ambrosia to the Passionate. Those Who Accomplish Are Not Slaves to Complacency.

Don Crist...

The President Must Not Allow the Thorn of the Rose to Diminish Its Sweet Scent

Often, presidents spend an inordinate amount of time and energy dwelling on the negative, and do not take the time to enjoy the positive.

Most people in the community do recognize the good work being done and support the college because of it. Presidents should recognize this and stop and pause to savor the sweet scent of the rose.

Gain the Home Field Advantage by Knowing the Ballpark

The smart president, early in his/her tenure, learns the nuances of the college district and how to function within it. Familiarity with the turf builds confidence in the leader. The more the president knows about the college district and the power brokers within it, the better prepared she/he will be to make the best decisions. The great sluggers could hit home runs and carry strong batting averages in any "hitters" ballpark. The president, who knows his district better than anyone, will make the best decisions and enjoy a more successful tenure as president, because he has gained the advantage of hitting in a "hitters" ballpark.

One Personal Attribute in the President's Toolbox That Is Used in Every Successful Effort Is Persistence; Two Others Are Persistence and Persistence

At times a president must choose a course of action that requires persistence if she/he is to be successful. In some situations it is easier to back off an issue rather than go the extra mile in developing necessary data and research. It is at these times persistence can make the difference between success and failure for the president.

Although a President Must Play the Hand Dealt, As the Game Progresses the President Is Entitled to Reshuffle the Deck

New presidents inherit the administrative team and the issues and initiatives of the previous president. You do have a window of opportunity to reshuffle the deck early in your tenure, but don't wait too long. Surround yourself with YOUR team and establish YOUR priorities in consultation with YOUR board. They may or may not include all persons and initiatives of the previous administration. It is okay and it is expected—everyone wants and needs for you to succeed. You will need all the help you can get. You and your team have to be on the same page.

The President, Like the Apple Farmer, Must Pick the Ripe Ones, Nurture the Green Ones, and Discard the Rotten Ones

Often the president cannot establish the best priorities and ends up picking too many apples from the tree. When this happens there are always going to be the good ones mixed up with the bad ones. If relatively new in the position, the president may win the early battles and nourish the good apples, but lose the war trying to save the bad apples. Make certain you determine your priorities based on solid advice and counsel, make certain they are obtainable, and make certain everyone knows what they are.

One Strike and You Might Be Out

It is often the little things that have the greatest impact on the relationship between the president and the board. Do not underestimate the effect of a disgruntled dignitary who was treated poorly while on campus, or the impact of a dirty vehicle used to transport board members to an off-site function.

Keep an eye on the seemingly small stuff, that some will characterize as micro-management. It doesn't matter the audience, the college must do the presentation flawlessly; the college catalog cannot have errors; ceremonies must start on time; the campus must be kept looking very well cared for; the college fleet must be clean inside and out; college guests must be looked after at all times, and on and on.

Remember, the president is the one the board will ask to fix things; that is, if they mention it at all. Unfortunately, board members tend not to bring these types of issues to the president and may harbor ill will. And when trustees begin to harbor ill will, the president may become, "one strike and you are out."

We Think We Can, We Know We Can

Whether by incremental "baby steps" or by "leaps and bounds" the transition of the college community from a WE THINK WE CAN to WE KNOW WE CAN mentality is the responsibility of the president.

The college community, likened to the train in *The Little Engine That Could*, must have the confidence and expectation of success if the president is to fulfill the mission of the institution.

The Presence of the President Is Usually More Important Than the President Perceives It to Be

All too often presidents do not take the time to attend meetings. It is not acceptable when the president continuously sends a stand-in or no one at all to meetings that are college specific. And to attend meetings with peers only on occasion can be a negative and a poor reflection on the president and the college he represents. Conversely, when the president does show up, is on time, takes part in discussion, and shows a genuine interest in the topic, a message is sent that this group is important and its work is valued. Remember, showing up is half the battle.

—WAYNE GREEN, Trustee, Carl Sandburg College

Chuck Novak…

A Leader Who Appreciates Is a Leader Who Is Appreciated

Leaders who are appreciated by the people they lead are the type of people who give the appreciation first. They appreciate people and their contributions to the organization. They recognize the worth of employee contributions, and they know how to genuinely say, "Thank you." Watching them work to improve the organization and its service to others is joyful.

Leadership and Self-Gratification Are Incompatible

Gratification is the joyful result of organizational performance, not individual performance—particularly the performance of the leader. People make an organization effective; good leadership encourages and inspires the people to make it happen.

Good Leadership Creates a Secure Environment

People will not communicate openly, let alone work together if they do not feel safe. They need to know the rules and expectations of the workplace (personnel policies). In a stable workplace there are clear organizational structures and employee roles and responsibilities are defined (organization of activity).

A secure employee is more comfortable with change and in seeking to improve process and performance. It is easier to embrace change and strengthen productivity when they have a sense of security.

Leadership is Every One Being Involved

Good leadership recognizes that often groups create better solutions than individuals working alone. Leadership learns the talents and abilities of the people who comprise the organization, and brings them together for a harmonious outcome. It is called creating organizational energy.

Leadership is Action Biased and Learns from Mistakes

Good leadership makes things happen. It is entrepreneurial and self motivated. It hides from nothing and is always alert to opportunity. Good leadership does not ignore a mistake, but will use it to teach how to not make the mistake again.

Chapter Five

EMPLOYEE RELATIONS

After students, employees are the greatest asset the college has. They do the work. They serve people. They create new programs. They find better ways to serve, to help, to educate. The college's employees are the character and the substance which creates institutional personality and success.

John Anderson...

The Drama of Employee Relations Is Like the Dance of a Porcupine and a Skunk

Employee relations are not confined to management and labor; they occur between and among all employees, individuals and groups. Each is prepared to announce that he is armed and dangerous, so tread lightly. This is apparently based on the pervasive assumption that every entreaty is a threat. Replacing the assumption of threat (adversarial) with the assumption of peace (alliance) is the small task of leadership. A leader often begins by suggesting that, "I am not against you; rather, it is you and I against the problem." People must find ways to establish trust and alliance, so they may dance comfortably together. To do this requires not only time and effort, but willingness. Sometimes, you must begin again, start over, get everyone together on square one and build from the bottom up with plain, simple talk. It must be made clear that all employees and employee groups have an equal right to participate, and that no one group has more importance than another.

Don Crist...

Making Light at Others Expense, No Matter How Good Natured the Intent, Will Damage the President and Hinder His or Her Ability to Lead.

There is a difference in appropriate behavior for the president and anyone else employed by the college. The president cannot make chiding comments at others' expense, even when those comments are intended to be good natured.

While Perceptions of the President May Be Accurate or Inaccurate, They Are Real to the Perceivers, and Are Rarely the Same as Those of the President

Have you noticed that in most fitness centers the walls are mirrors from floor to ceiling? It is shocking to most who are working out for the first time to see themselves that "up close and personal." This experience usually causes people to work harder to get the new look they want and is a regular reminder of your fitness progress. For the president to have the same daily and weekly "heads up" on how the college community sees the president, he must communicate effectively with all employee groups regularly. The constant feedback from these groups will be like looking into the wall of mirrors and keeping the president in touch with the internal community.

Chuck Novak...

When It Comes To Employee Relations, There Is Always a Communication Problem

Regardless of the style of leadership, there are always communication problems. People want information about the organization. Good leadership accepts the communication "problem" unconditionally. Communication deals with questions such as: "What are we doing and what is our purpose?" "What's going on and who is doing it?" "How are we doing? And thank you for your understanding." Good leadership broadcasts to all.

All and Part Should Not Be Adversaries, but Often They Are

Seeing Part of an enterprise will lead to a particular set of conclusions, opinions and attitudes. Seeing All of the enterprise will lead to another broader set of conclusions, opinions and attitudes. The two perspectives will be different and can lead to points of conflict. In an education enterprise, with all of its disciplines and vocations, there are many venues and opportunities for difference. All and Part are components of the same enterprise, and when they fail to get along, when they come into conflict, it is because they fail to see each other. It is incumbent upon the All to help the Parts see the All.

Money Is Good, Esteem Is Better

Everybody cares about money, and too much is not enough. But money does not replace a personal feeling of worth and being appreciated. Unless they are being exploited, employees will trade some money for knowing they are part of the total enterprise and that their contributions make the enterprise better than it was. It is critical to avoid treating one employee differently than another or a group of employees differently than another employee group. This drives wedges and causes dissension; apply both rules and privileges equally.

The Students Are Why We Are There, But About Employees, You Better Care

Change a set of personnel policies without broad consideration, or engage in a protracted and unruly dispute with an employee union, and it is the students who will pay. There may be proclamations from disputants that "students come first," that they would never "harm students in any way." The leader who believes that is naïve. Experienced leaders know that the manner in which they conduct business with employees will always impact students.

It Is Not Stability, It Is Security

A secure employee can be changing daily, performing better and finding better ways to serve. Employees have a desire and a responsibility to know and understand the expectations of the workplace. They need to understand the nature of their work and the rules they must follow when working. When they are secure, it is less threatening for them to embrace change and improve productivity.

In the Community College Unions Are Becoming a Way of Life, but With the Right Kind of Leadership They Need Not Be the Best Way of Life

The ripe ground for unions is in the government and utility sectors. Education is a government sector, and the unions protect teachers and other employees from change, and sometimes from themselves. So unions have an attraction to employees who are insecure. And if you are a state without right to work laws, there is probably an organizational movement somewhere on the premises; this is often followed by a union chapter. Or, leadership may accept responsibility for all the institution's employees and compete with the union for their loyalty. Doing that takes courage and patience.

When the Union Comes; You Will Know Their Every Move

Don't ask; don't snoop; it is not needed. Unless leadership has disaffected every employee in the organization, leadership will be informed. The leader who has faith in the employees will find employees who have faith in the leader.

Never Malign a Union Organization Campaign

Work with it. Understand it. Challenge it with facts and proven observations. Write informative letters in the third person to employees about the issues the union raises. Be informative, not partial. Write facts. Opinions have no place in this debate. And, never behave like you are in a fight, even though you may be.

Write To Employees and Have a Real Reason to Do So

The president must write to employees, but only in response to a union letter or actual concerns which have been expressed by employees to the CEO. Do not write if there is nothing requiring a response no matter how compelling. Responding informatively to real, expressed concerns insures that the employees who expressed the concern will discuss the response, appreciate it, and, perhaps, legitimize it.

Ask Employees for the Right to Represent Them

After all, you are their employer, and they are your greatest asset. Ask in the first person, and say who is asking for the right to represent them—the president, the board and the college administration. There is nothing wrong with being straight forward. If the president does not ask, the employees may conclude no one cares.

Never Make a Pejorative Remark about a Union

Criticism of a union gives it traction. Acknowledge the union's right to organize and represent the employees. Discuss issues, not the union. Stick with the issues and facts, and constantly clarify the unionization and representation process—the rules and procedures.

Stay Visible and Ask All for Civility

In every letter and in the first person, always end by asking for civility. There are thousands of ways to ask for civility, and every request of civility counts for something good.

Chapter Six

THE EXTERNAL PRESIDENT: THE POLITICS OF RELATIONSHIPS

John Anderson...

In the End There Is Naught but That Which You Had by Relationship with Others

Don Crist...

The President Must Not Confuse Issues with Allies

Your allies may differ with you on certain issues. Don't be confused by their challenges, for they, in the end, are likely to be among your supporters—as long as you listen to their point of view and you are open to their suggestions in making decisions. Allies are allies, and issues don't divide them.

If the President Doesn't Ask for Money—the College Won't Get It

The odds of passing a referendum that would raise taxes are dismal at best. States in general have not funded community colleges in the manner intended. The community college president has been forced to spend a lot of time fund raising and working with the college foundation. In essence he is becoming like his/her private college counterpart.

Many presidents didn't think raising money, asking for donations, and spending a lot of time with a foundation would be a primary responsibility of president. They were focused on building programs, building facilities to house programs, and expanding opportunities for students.

Fund raising is an important function of the presidency. A president must consider that as part of the NEAT stuff that all dream of doing as presidents. Yes, it is the president's job, and one the president cannot and will not delegate to others in the organization.

Only another President May Serve As a Person with Whom to Be Completely and Safely Candid

Presidents are the only ones who walk in the shoes of presidents. To assume that trustees, vice-presidents, and community leaders can provide the advice most presidents need from time to time is a fallacy. Presidents who confide in persons other than Presidents are throwing the dice. Pick up the phone and call the neighboring college president when you need to talk to someone.

When the President Becomes Involved in the Election of a Board Member, It Is Time to Begin Preparing for the Next Job

One of the basic rules of college administration is stay out of board politics. We all learn this and take it for granted until, until, until....

I doubt there is a president who, at some time in his or her tenure, isn't tempted to support and campaign for one board candidate over another. Even when one candidate is against the administration and the other candidate is a friend of the administration, you must not get involved. For those who do this, it is the beginning of the end, regardless of the outcome of the election. DO NOT make this mistake, and if you do cross the line, start looking for your next job.

The President Is Cautioned Not to Schedule Too Many Away Games as Internal and External Presence Must Be in Balance

Many professional organizations rely on successful presidents to provide leadership at the local, state, and national levels. This, of course is a compliment to the president, and he/she should do that which is important to him and his board. However, the president is cautioned to stay close to his internal and external customers, not relinquish a preponderance of decision making to subordinates, and recognize that both the college and professional organizations seeking his help will be there whether he is or not.

The President is always the President

The actions of the president are always looked upon as a reflection of the college. The president is always the president: at the grocery store, the basketball game, the fitness center, or coffee shop. The president does not own his time like most other individuals in the community and cannot enjoy that luxury. The president is the leader of the college community, and must emulate that image always.

The community and the board of trustees often look upon the president as "the college."

Chuck Novak…

It Is All Relationships

For a college president there is no such thing as "by yourself." With the exception of the president's personal manner and conduct, everything else requires assistance and guidance from other people. There are people everywhere—board members, community members, legislators, bureaucrats, local office holders, faculty, students, governors; everywhere there are people who matter. There is no escape from building relationships. Of course, a president may choose not to build a relationship here or there, but there will still be a relationship. Someone else will build it, and the outcome will be uncertain.

A college president should be cautioned against functioning as a committee of one. Rarely, does the president make a decision absent of influence by board members, students, employees, business/community leaders, politicians or others. Today, a president simply cannot be successful when acting in isolation. It is expected that the president will build and nurture strong relationships with all entities that can help support the mission of the college.

The relationships which the president grows with constituent groups will define the manner in which the college, its activities and its future are viewed by both the general public and the college's employees.

The Tail Must Not Wag the Dog: a Lawyer Is a Lawyer, Is a Lawyer, and By Any Other Name Is Still a Tail

Never take orders from someone you pay by the hour. Lawyers, architects, engineers, and other specialists are not employed to replace the president or usurp the wisdom of the board of trustees. Specialists interpret circumstances from a narrower point of view. Values, vision, purpose and what is best for students are the concerns of generalists. The president and members of the board are the chief generalists who must engage considerations which are all encompassing. Specialists advise generalists about how to achieve what the organization needs to achieve, not whether the achievement is worthy. The president must see the whole picture, interpret the whole picture, and make decisions that advance the whole picture.

You Are a Lobbyist Whether You Like It or Not

If there is something the college needs, the president will need to lobby to get it. A new road to the college means the president needs the help of the mayor and enough votes on the city council. A new building means the president needs the approval of the required state agencies and the necessary appropriation from the legislature. The lobbying starts at the front door of the college and winds the roads to city hall, the state capitol and Washington D.C. Rarely will an elected official ask the president what the college needs; everybody needs something. Why stir them up? The president must ask for the college to receive.

Elected Officials Always Stick.......Together

Elected officials are who they are because they have developed and cultivated a base of public support. They run for office for various reasons, but the reasons are irrelevant when it comes to their kinship with one another. Their kinship grows from the fact that they all did the same thing. They organized, they ran, and they won. They talk to each other, and they listen to each other. Should you decide that one is not particularly effective, it is likely that all will soon learn of your feelings. Should you decide that their work is not as noble as is the work of the college, it is likely all will soon learn of your definition. Should you decide public officials are to be informed and appreciated, it is likely that all will know, and they will help.

Bring Them on the Campus Close to Students

Elected officials run for office, we hope, because they believe they can make a difference. They want to contribute and they want to have impact. They may become bogged down in political processes they often do not appreciate, but they keep working to make the difference. There is no better place to see this difference than a community college campus. Introduce them often, and stay out of their way so they can relate directly with students. They will become friends of the college and they will have the college in common.

Never Ignore, Underestimate, or Fail to Understand a State Agency

Community colleges are, in part instruments of the State. The rules are different from state to state, but the reality is the same. State agencies control or influence the funding, operations, building programs, and various types of certifications. Sometimes state agencies are a nuisance to everyone, and presidents must band together to blunt their impact. Everything is subject to political pressure applied appropriately, and democracy works best when the state is afraid of the people.

Simple, Soft Persistence Is Aggression Tolerated

Nothing comes if nothing is sought. The secret to sustaining success lies in the manner in which one seeks. Some will scream, complain, and object, and others will moan of discrimination or special treatment; they occasionally get something, but nobody likes giving it to them. Then there are others who appear to live under a rain tree in the spring, the leaves always turning gold. These are the people who know their relationships and the influence that precipitates as a consequence. The president asks. They ask quietly, and often, and receive. Though relentless, they are always pleasant.

There Is Only One Allegiance, the College

When the people see the president, they think of the college. When they hear the president, they learn about the college. The college and the president are one. The president eschews political preferences. His only cause is the college. If you exhibit a political preference or align with an external cause, your image is altered. People start taking sides and the college is not the same anymore.

While Friends May Come and Go, Your Enemies Accumulate (anonymous)

For the college president with long tenure: While your friends are mostly going, your enemy's friends accumulate.

Chapter 7

THE WORKINGS OF THE BOARD OF TRUSTEES

No organization is any better than its board of directors; no college is any better than its board of trustees. The board can hire an experienced college president with a long record of success, but if the board does not function at a high level of consciousness, the president's best efforts will be reduced to mediocrity. On the other hand, a cohesive board which has high standards and expectations and knows how to express and evaluate those expectations can help a president be more effective. The board must support the president, and the president must support the board

The Board of Trustees and the President Must Fly Five Miles Above, and Five Years Ahead of the Organization They Lead

It is customarily the role of the president to inspire the formation of a vision for the college. He must, in concert with trustees, and with input from the campus and community, envision the future. The board and the president must lead the college into its next phase of distinction, and marshal its resources in support of this end. An unobstructed view of the future is required.

—JOHN AHERN, Trustee, Black Hawk College

John Anderson...

The Board: A Two-Way Window for the College

The board is largely responsible for the public's view of the college. The board is largely responsible for the college's view of the public. It is, therefore, imperative that the board be comprised of highly competent and dedicated trustees; trustees who are wholly, not specifically, committed to the college's outcomes.

Boards must police their own ranks and seek candidates who will, decidedly, not be single-issue members; who are not politically motivated; who do not represent any one special interest group, or sub-public within the college's district.

Incumbent trustees should actively recruit new members from the community who have been successful in their fields of endeavor, and who are thoughtful and intelligent, respected, knowledgeable, and honest. Nothing less will do for our community colleges whose product will be increasingly vital to the community's future.

Every Which Way but One

The president's responsibility is to operate the college in an effective and efficient way. The board's responsibility is to help the president accomplish it. It's easy! Unless, of course, the board is regularly divided, resulting in what is called a "split board." This is characterized as a predictable division among the members. Issues and actions are either supported or opposed by the same sub-groups within the Board. This circumstance is difficult for the president, and counterproductive for the college; if the president does not receive clear direction, needed actions can languish unresolved. The chair and the president must develop strategies to help all members of the board resolve differences and regain cohesiveness. Certainly, differences of opinion and approach are acceptable, even desirable. But, there eventually must be resolution followed by acceptance and support by all members of the board.

Two Heads Are Better Than One, but Not on the Same Person

The relationship between a board chair and president is unique and unlike the president's relationship with other board members. It is crucial that the president and board chair work well as a team. The board chair can be a sounding board to the president on things such as issues, policies and direction. The same can be said of the president to the board chair. He can help support the board chair with his knowledge and experience.

—RANDY SCHAEFER, Trustee, Rock Valley College

Don Crist...

Personal Relationships with Community and Business Leaders Can Be Good and Bad; Good When Their Influence Helps the College; Bad When Your Influence Helps Them

In small communities it is easy for the president to develop close personal relationships with community leaders identified with a particular group. Remember, you must stay above the fray in order to be an effective leader.

The President Must Remember That Off-The-Record Comments with the Media Are Never Off-The-Record

Do not think there is ever an "off-the-record" discussion with the media. Presidents live and work in a fish bowl, and they must recognize and accept that media will disappoint you on occasion. Be cautioned to be discrete in your comments. Say no more than is necessary regardless of how passionate you feel about an issue.

The President Should Make Every Decision as Though He Was In a Public Board Meeting

The administration must have their "ducks in line" with every recommendation they make that requires board action. The president should give the same consideration to all decisions he or she makes, regardless of whether it requires board approval or not.
—Lanny Rudd, Dean (retired), Carl Sandburg College

The President Must Possess the Ability and Insight to Move the College from the Comfort Zone to the Extraordinary

Regardless of the status of the college, the president must have the leadership ability to move the institution forward. College communities and boards do become complacent and satisfied with the status quo when things are going well. It is at these times the president must step forward and lead the college from comfort to the extraordinary; it is these times that provide the greatest opportunity for those who lead; it is these times that provide the legacy for most Presidents.

When the Board Chair Makes a Suggestion…the President Should Regard It as More than a Suggestion

When the board chair calls and says, "You may want to consider painting the Board Room," get the paint crew together and paint the Board Room. When the board chair calls and says "You might want to take a second look at Item "X" on this month's board agenda," take Item "X" off the agenda until you have met and discussed the rationale for it with the board chair.

In each instance the board chair was not really suggesting that you consider these things. He or she was telling you to change it, unless you could provide a rationale for going forward. Reading the board is one of those lessons a president must learn early in his or her tenure as president.

When The Board's Evaluation of the President Is Reduced to Merely a Check List of Specific Expectations, the President Might Be Advised to Freshen Her Or His Resume

Evaluations of the president vary a great deal from college to college. Mostly, the evaluation process is positive, and is an evaluation of both the president and of the board of trustees. It is not good when the president's evaluation becomes a check-off list of expectations. If this occurs, the president is advised to begin thinking about a change.

In most instances presidents know when it is a good time to make a change, and will do so before it is deemed necessary by the trustees. Seldom do presidents get blind-sided. Evaluations provide insight and avenues for growth for both president and board.

An Experienced President Knows That If She Acts In Ways That Harm the College...Responsible Trustees Will Fire the President, Regardless of the Strength of Their Relationship

Trustees as a whole are extremely protective of the college and will not hesitate to take action against anyone that poses a threat to the institution. The president, regardless of her relationship with board members is not exempt, if not acting in the best interest of the college. Know that every decision you make needs to be in the best interest of the students you serve.

Chuck Novak...

Communication "with" the Board—Communication "about" the Board

Communication "with" the board means among, in association with, in cooperation with. It implies a relationship and a partnership, by working together.

Communication "about" the board means in relation to, in reference to, pertaining to and in regard to all of the board's expectations, deliberations and activities.

No Institution Is Any Better Than Its Board of Directors

It doesn't make any difference if it is a bank, a major corporation, or a community college. The board of trustees establishes the environment for the entire institution. If an institution has a poor board, even the best chief executive officer will never succeed to achieve what could be achieved if the board was effective.

Effective Boards Do Not Just Happen, They Become

Few things in life just come naturally, and when a skill or talent is natural, it can still be honed. Distinctive talents, abilities and achievements are a result of focused learning. For the learning to occur there needs to be a teacher. When it comes to board development, the college president often may be the primary teacher, not the only teacher, but the primary teacher. It is in the job description.

Board Member Orientation Is Not a Nuisance

The college president who eschews the responsibility for board orientation will pay for it and maybe never know why. Being a trustee for a complex organization is a tough job, especially for the trustee who understands the complexity of the organization. Allow a trustee to be uninformed and the trustee will think the job simple and undemanding. The president's job will be more difficult.

Never Anticipate a Board Meeting

Board meetings, by their very nature, can be totally unpredictable. The unexpected can always happen and the anticipated may never happen. There is no way to know the future, and the imagination can create futures that are bizarre at best. Being in the board meeting itself is far less difficult than anticipating what may or may not happen in it. Prepare the board material thoroughly, mail it in plenty of time, and focus on the day after.

Only Fight with a Board Member in Public during the Board Meeting

For every college president, the day of the clash will come. Keep it in the sunshine. Focus on the issues, do the research, and present the case impersonally. No one else will do it; no one will help you, especially another board member. It is the president's issue even if it is a college wide issue; the president is the person who will have to stand the line. Do it. Honesty, integrity, courage and sunshine in the same package never need a stamp to be delivered.

The Whole World Needs to Know What the Board Is, What It Does, How It Works, and Who Its Members Are

Everyone knowing ABOUT the board is as important as the relationship between the board and the CEO—almost. Board members need to be able to enjoy serving the college and meeting its people, and the college's people need to see the board work as well as enjoy its members' company. The board has the authority and autonomy to be original, creative and regenerative; that is its responsibility. To arrive there, at distinctiveness, the board needs to be in the veins of the place to feel the flow and choose the directions.

Board Members Have But One Allegiance: The Entire Institution and Its Purpose

Board members who think their role is to represent special constituencies dilute trust and undermine institutional mission. It only takes one. All the others are distracted from moving to a higher level of consciousness. The halls come alive with gamesmanship until the episode is worn and fades to nothing. But there will be another episode.

Individuals Do Not Make Board Decisions

Every board is made up of individuals who embrace and promote differing beliefs. Each individual has different associations, loyalties and preferences. Therefore, debate and differing opinions are to be expected and often encouraged. However, all the individual expressions need to be heard with the knowledge in mind that there are no individual decisions. Board decisions are team decisions.

Some Board Members Must Be Endured

The board member was wrong. The meeting went two hours longer than needed; everybody knew it. But, the college president who commits a patience slip, verbal or not verbal, will eventually pay for it. Endure and educate. Some board members take more time. Give it; it's called board development. Endure and Educate. Facilitate. Teach.

Some Board Members Must be Enjoyed

They have a moral core and the experience which built it. They have been around. They have given to others. They may not fight for you, but they will always offer advice. They never turn anyone away. Keep their company and drink their wisdom. Never take them for granted for they are like everyone else. To support the president, they need to know the why and the what of the president's doings.

Chapter 8

WHO WILL LEAD? SHADES OF THE ALMIGHTY

Announcements for college presidents often seem to ask for the impossible. We want someone who can walk on water without scaring the fish, someone who will write our prayers but let us say, "Amen." The pool of qualified candidates for college presidencies has decreased in recent years. A few years ago it was not uncommon to receive 100 applications in response to announcements for a presidential search, most of which were qualified. Today, 30-40 applications are more likely, with some of those not meeting all of the qualifications. Why?

John Anderson...

We Have Made the Job Unfairly Difficult to Get

The search and selection process is cumbersome and works poorly. Far too many people are involved (the search committee) with special interest conditions that are often in opposition to one another and unrelated to the college's mission. The board usually has no involvement with the applicants until they receive 3-5 finalists. Good applicants whom the board may have preferred have already been eliminated by employees or other committee members with personal agendas. The board must regain control from start to finish and reserve the right to interview any or none of the applicants. Also, the early intrusion of the media into the process discourages top "prospects" from applying. Efforts by the media to identify, and scrutinize all applicants is a disservice to the college, the public, and the applicant. The public need to know is adequately served by identifying only the final candidates to be interviewed. If necessary, legislation should be sought to reduce harassment, and to protect privacy rights of applicants.

We Have Made the Job Unfairly Difficult to Keep

Everyone has been allowed to attack the president and tell him how to do the job. The president has a 360 degree circle of potential antagonists: employees, media, trustees, public, students, government and special interest groups. They feel "entitled" to criticize the president, while the president, curiously, is not allowed to respond. Boards must have the grit to ignore the noise level and ascertain if there is any substance to the criticism. Sometimes, the majority of employees do not agree with the criticism but, unfortunately, they remain silent. A particular caution to the board is to be wary of the so-called "vote of no confidence" tactic. The more credence it is given by boards, the more often it will be used. Or, perhaps boards should establish a policy which allows these "votes of no confidence" to be used universally within the college. It helps to be reminded of the fact that the president reports to the board and only the board. The president is the board's only employee. Everyone else that works at the college reports to the president. It is crucial that the board support the president openly and strongly until it cannot; then the Board must replace the president.

We Do Not Compensate the President Adequately

It is a difficult job and doesn't pay well. Most companies in the private sector with budgets comparable to a community college compensate their CEO's substantially more than is paid a community college president. The president is not, and should not be, a part of the wage structures used for the college in general. The other college officers may also be considered separately for compensation as recommended by the president. Be proud enough of your executive staff to pay them adequately, or replace them.

We May Not Find the Devotion in Today's Environment

Despite the harassment and modest pay, presidents have been devoted warriors who wanted to serve in these important positions because they loved it and believed in it and had a passion for it. Today's applicants may be more practical and less idealistic.

Nothing Prepares You to Be President Like Being President

A vice-president once asked what the main difference was between being president and vice-president. The president replied, when you go home tonight you might ask, I wonder what "he" will do about a certain matter; when the president goes home, he must ask, what "I" will do about a certain matter.

Courage Revisited

In the exercise of courage, we must respect the process, but champion the outcome; the outcome is achieving the mission. In the end, process is servant to product. The board, with advice from the president, assures that the right thing is being done; the board then relies on the president to see that the thing is done right, i.e., leadership and management.

Some things the board or president must do are neither fun nor popular; have the courage to do them in either case. If you are criticized for it, do it anyway. Always ask, "Will what we intend to do benefit students?" If the answer is yes, do it.

Don Crist...

There Is a Body of Knowledge about Community Colleges, and Their Leaders Can Be Cultivated and Prepared

There are numerous graduate programs for preparing educational administrators, but relatively few are dedicated to the community college. Community college presidents, and other administrators, are unique and different from their counterparts in the universities and the public schools. Those who desire to become a community college president should seek out programs with major emphasis on the community college. College boards are advised to look for candidates who have completed degrees from universities with community college specific programs. The universities are advised to work more closely with community colleges to (1) develop effective curricula, (2) provide internship opportunities, and (3) employ currently practicing or retired college administrators to teach courses in the graduate programs.

Presidents Have Stories to Tell

Most presidents have a story to tell…a story that embodies the community college movement. The stories that candidates for the presidency have to tell should be given consideration in the selection process. These stories revolve around the second and third chances in life, the late bloomers, overcoming financial roadblocks to secure an education, the right vocational choices, scholarships and grants, or the working student. These tests produce individuals who have the "makings" for becoming a college president. Sometimes those who have the makings do not consider themselves to be presidential material. They must be identified and encouraged if we are to get the best applicants for these important positions.

Chuck Novak…

Keeping Community in the Community College

Involving the college community in a presidential search can be good or not so good; it depends upon how you involve them. If the board abandons the process, the results will be the product of competing interests, bias and compromise. However, if the board involves the college community in developing a profile of the kind of president needed to move the college forward, and structures the process accordingly, the results can be excellent. Board members must stay involved with the search advisory committee and with the consultants they may have hired to direct the search. The college community should then be respectful of the board's responsibility and authority to select the next president.

John Anderson . . .

Indeed, Who Will Lead?

A recent study from Iowa State University conducted by Chris Duree, documents a community college leadership shortage looming in the near-term future. It was found that 79 percent of community college presidents will retire by 2012, and 84 percent by 2016. The study also reports that the number of degrees awarded to graduates of community college leadership programs decreased by 78 percent between 1983 and 2007.

"So, actually, not only is there the anticipated exodus going out the door, but there is also the shortage of qualified candidates coming in," Duree said.

The data was collected in 2007 by a group of researchers in the Department of Educational Leadership and Policy Studies and the Office of Community College Research and Policy at Iowa State University.

Chapter 9

OTHER MUSINGS AND OBSERVATIONS

There are some other thoughts which the authors wished to include in this guide; however, they did not lend themselves to the aphoristic style. Therefore, they are included as short essays and observations. They deal with such topics as presidential tenure, president and board relations, and the primary responsibility of a governing board.

John Anderson...

Student Success Is the Highest and Best Expression of the College's Mission

The most important activity at the college is learning, and the students do that. Therefore, everyone that works at the college, both operational and teaching staff, provide support service to learning (students).

Student Services—A Full, Professional Partner

It is the prerogative and responsibility of the president to determine the administrative makeup of the college. Student Services, as a division of the college, is vital to the mission of the college through its focus on student development and success.

A mistake sometimes made in the organizational structure of community colleges is the placement of Student Services as an add-on to Instructional Services. First, it is a basic conflict of interest for the Vice President of Instructional Services to administer Student Services. Second, it relegates Student Services and, therefore, students to a second class status within the organization. It stifles the voice speaking for students in many regards, and sends a message that Student Services is not a priority equal to that of Instructional Services and other areas represented by a vice president. Student Services is a legitimate division of the college and should have a chief administrative officer.

The Board and the President: A Symbiosis

The president must exercise a set of responsibilities in his duty to SERVE the board. The board must exercise a set of responsibilities in its duty to SUPPORT the president. These responsibilities need to be well understood so that the board and president are defined as a strong and unified force working to achieve the mission of the college.

What the President "Owes" the Board:

- Valid credentials and qualifications
- High energy and strong spirit
- Honesty and integrity
- Sound advice
- A passion for the enterprise; commitment is not enough
- Actions that represent the will of the Board, and not individual members
- Loyalty and respect

What the Board "Owes" the President:

> Unwavering devotion to the mission of the college
> Warriors for securing resources
> Informed about trends and issues for community colleges
> Cohesiveness—function as a Board and not as individuals
> A healthy disinterest in specific personnel or budget matters
> Honesty and integrity
> Support and trust

Don't Be at the Airport When Your Ship Comes In (Anonymous)

Public organizations with elected boards are not always able to act as quickly or decisively as private organizations, and are sometimes accused of missing opportunities or suffering long delays. On occasion, it is due to their own failings, but more often it is due to the nature of public organizations and the constraints under which they must operate.

Some will argue that the most important responsibility of a governing board is to define the mission of the institution. That is true, but it will only hold true if the board hires a chief executive that can carry out the mission successfully. Like the corporate CEO, the college president personifies the institution, and is the board's executive officer. He is recognized as the leader of the institution both internally and externally. The Board has the sole responsibility to govern the institution and set the policies to be implemented by the president and administration. Policies have a clear role; they provide oversight to the plan that embraces the general goals to be implemented by the president. The president acts for, and is under, the direction of the board of trustees; this relationship must be understood by everyone who is associated with the institution. It is the responsibility of the board to give the president the support he needs to carry out their policies and directives. In short, the board governs and the president manages. The board supports its CEO until it can no longer do so. If that point is reached, the Board and President have a responsibility to themselves and each other to part company in a professional manner.

—STEVE SPIVEY, former Board Chair, Black Hawk College

Don Crist...

Bigger Is Always Bigger, But Not Always Better

In some states minimum size is one of the threshold requirements for a community college district. District resident and student populations may be among the criteria for the establishment of a community college district.

There should be a national discussion about what really constitutes minimum standard for a community college in the United States. Size would be given much less attention in the context of a national forum. We would most likely talk about the comprehensiveness of the programs, and if the college is meeting the needs of the citizenry. What matters? Size does not matter; service does.

Don't Buy Technology Just to Have Technology; Buy Function and Service

With the advent of distance learning, online courses, paperless learning centers, e-textbooks, and smart classrooms, it is reasonable to expect the President to be ahead of the curve. All presidents do not need to be computer geeks; however, the president must have a working knowledge of the instructional technology of the present and the future.

Take the time to become computer literate. Learn the programs utilized by your faculty and students, and the administrators. Set the example and the standard for the college employees and the board. Provide laptops and move to a paperless campus as fast as you can. Do this with the press, and communicate internally and externally through the electronic media. Eliminate board mailings yesterday, and implement electronic communication with the Board.

Do this for your students, and the college will be better for it.

Tuition Is Tuition Is Tuition—By Any Other Name Is the Same Amount

Charge a fair tuition and advertise it that way. Charging extra fees for various reasons in order to avoid the discussion about tuition increases and justification is not necessary. We have all rented a car at an advertised price of say $49.95 a day only to discover that the true cost was $69.95 a day due to extra fees. One-stop shopping with one bottom line price is always the best approach; you will like it and so will the students.

To Be a Resident or a Vagabond President; That Is the Question and the Answer

Either choice or circumstance will determine the answer to this question. Both are important. The "vagabond" president moves from college to college and is generally an agent of change. The "resident" president may stay at one or two colleges for an entire career and is a stabilizing force on most college campuses.

Take the path best suited to your administrative style, and never look back. Both types of presidents have a place in most colleges, and do great work in moving an organization forward. Seek out the presidency that is a good fit for you; it is your call, and a decision you must not take lightly.

The Cart before the Horse...No Matter...They Are the Same

It is because we have tended to the business of our students that the community college has evolved into the "people's college." Do not forget that students always come first and that we cannot and should not replicate the universities. We are about students and community...they are the cart and the horse.

Anderson/Crist/Novak . . .

Respecting the Necessary Divisions of Labor in a Community College Will Ensure That The College Continues to Serve the People

It has been our privilege to have worked with many outstanding people in the community college. These colleagues, both teaching and non-teaching staff, are bright, qualified and dedicated to students and the mission of the college. They stay current in their field, are willing to go the extra mile, and contribute to developing and implementing a plan for the future of the college. We salute this majority of colleagues for being a credit to their profession, and they must be excused from the following discussion.

Community Colleges need to revisit the divisions of labor for employees so trustees can maintain control of their institutions. For colleges to be creative and innovative in developing new programs and services to meet emerging demands, employees must focus on the work they have been assigned and for which they are qualified.

Teachers and other employee groups have become increasingly engaged in the governance and management of the institution. They accomplish this more by aggressive influence than by specific authority. Consensus is healthy and should be promoted, but it does not replace responsibility.

Trustees are given the responsibility and authority for the colleges they serve by the citizens through election and by state statute. Another kind of authority/responsibility is that given by being hired to perform certain work assignments such as teaching, administration, and counseling, etc. A third kind of authority/responsibility is qualification by appropriate credential. In this case an employee possesses a body of knowledge and associated skill commonly referred to as a discipline such as biology, administration, information technology, engineering, etc. These disciplines all have equal integrity for their related work functions. The system has broken down because we have allowed employees from all the other disciplines to believe they are both qualified and entitled to practice the discipline of administration, and to govern. They are not. Nor, are they the ones who are responsible for the operations of the institution. It is the board and administration who are responsible and always accountable.

A history teacher should not necessarily be an administrator because (a) it is not his/her job assignment and (b) he/she is likely not qualified for this work. An administrator should not necessarily teach history for the same two reasons. Of course, there may be cases when an employee is qualified in both administration and pedagogy. However, the majority of employees are not, nor are they so qualified as groups of employees.

Another concern is that insurance companies are influencing the actions of boards and presidents by settling claims instead of going to court. In many instances, legal cost is the reason rather than the strength or merit of the case; this can be counterproductive and erodes the authority of the college board. To continue down this path may lead to control of community colleges by state government rather than local boards of trustees. Local boards might be appointed and advisory instead of elected and controlling. We should not want this to happen unless we believe that politicians have a better understanding of the needs of the community, and the role of the community college than a local board elected within a college district.

Today, employee factions have compromised trustees and presidents through procedural and confrontational tactics. This has minimized progress and, in some cases, prevented the Board from implementing goals for developing new programs and improving quality as well as from providing the accountability demanded by students, accrediting agencies and the public. State legislatures and boards of trustees are admonished to acknowledge this growing problem and empower the presidents and executive officers to, once again, run the college. If not, the grand mission of the community college may be forfeited and the next level of excellence and service for the people's college will not be realized.

-Closing Thoughts-

After many years in the saddle, and following much discussion, the authors have concluded that the path to success is paved with good leadership. Good leadership happens when a strong leader uses input from all of the stakeholders. So, people make it happen; people and leadership are the fundamental ingredients in success.

Not everyone can be "the leader", but everyone can participate in the leadership experience. The presidency is the natural and expected position to serve as leader. This role should, and generally is, respected and appreciated; however, we caution not to listen for noisy accolades.

We have a suggestion. There is a reservoir of talent and energy that is greatly underutilized. It is filled with retired presidents and trustees, many of whom would be willing to serve in advisory roles. This wealth of knowledge and experience must be used. We propose:

1. A national forum each year attended by college leaders, trustees, political leaders and community leaders. The agenda would be an honest dialogue about the important role of community colleges in helping to meet the challenges of our people and our nation. What are the issues? What are the solutions? The outcomes and recommendations could be prepared as a report and presented to government entities and congressional committees. These deliberations might result in actions that will benefit programming and students, and so, the economy and overall strength of our nation.

2. A system whereby new presidents and trustees could access former presidents and trustees to discuss specific issues affecting their colleges.......a life line when special help is needed. Contact

could be made via telephone, internet (a help desk), or on-site visitation. This approach may alleviate time and effort spent on solutions that have been previously resolved. A resource of this type would provide trustees and presidents with advice and counsel from trusted colleagues.

3. A nationwide plan to strengthen university programs in community college Administration and Leadership. This discipline must be current, relevant and practical in order to produce graduates who are well prepared.

The following strategies will help:

1. Utilize retired presidents as visiting and/or adjunct faculty and as field monitors and supervisors for internships at community colleges.

2. Appoint retired presidents as full-time faculty with non-tenured contracts for teaching and curriculum development in community college programs.

3. Require professors to do an internship at a community college every 3-5 years to keep updated. This can be worked out with many college boards and presidents.

4. Invite presidents and retired presidents to participate in community college graduate programs via distance education. Students would have access to the expertise of those who are practicing and those who have been successful as presidents.

Some universities have successfully strengthened the curricula for higher education doctoral programs designed for emerging community college professionals. The addition of more specific and practical courses is to be applauded. At the risk of redundancy, the authors suggest the following course topics for inclusion in community college doctoral programs.

Working with a locally elected board of trustees
Developing and managing a community college budget
Understanding facilities maintenance

Planning, funding and building new facilities
Student body profiles and providing access
Building community partnerships
Public relations and working with the media
Fund raising and the college foundation
Working with politicians and government organizations
The president's contract: terms and conditions
Inside the presidency

Again, the activation of these retired professionals would be selective by invitation. Some may have had all the fun they can stand. Those who participate will make an invaluable contribution. We challenge the leadership of our national organizations to strongly consider these propositions, and to enlist the author's assistance when needed.

This is our take on it and our effort to help those who are, or desire to become, college administrators. We have enjoyed identifying and attempting to explain the things that make a difference in your work. Needed, are education professionals who yearn for a vocational calling, and who will grow commitment into passion as they toil, unabashedly, to assure student success as prescribed by the college's mission and goals. Mostly, your reward will manifest as personal satisfaction, but, occasionally, it might be an epicurean delight from a petite portion of gratitude served up by a student, a colleague, a board or a community. Savor it. The profession must have bright, positive thinking people for its next generation of leaders, both instructional and operational. These leaders will need to give their best in order to fully represent and serve all who depend on the community college to provide general education along with career and life skills. These leaders must assure that the people's college remains what it was designed to be. This will be their challenge…our students and our communities deserve no less.

We wish you well for a long and productive career, and encourage you to take the community college to its next level of distinction; let it be your quest. Anderson, Crist and Novak will be your unflinching advocates, and we leave you with this one last aphorism.

John Anderson…

Always Leave Them Laughing

The budget is balanced, there are no lawsuits pending, the media is civil to you, you just passed a bond election, and the Board is pleased with your performance. It might be a good time to leave.

About the Authors...

JOHN H. ANDERSON was a teacher in Michigan before earning a masters degree from Arizona State University. He was a high school teacher, counselor and coach in Arizona. John then accepted a position at Northwestern Michigan College where he served for sixteen years in various Student Services positions and was an instructor in Astronomy. During this time he earned his doctorate degree in Higher Education Administration from ASU. He served in the positions of Dean of Instruction and Vice President of Instruction and Student Services at community colleges in Michigan and West Virginia before accepting the presidency at Northland Pioneer College in Arizona in 1991. After six years as president, John retired and represented NPC at the Arizona State Legislature for three years. John was honored to serve as President of the Arizona Community College President's Association and the Arizona Community College Association, and has been active in civic and professional organizations. John has completed interim presidencies at Black Hawk College and at Rock Valley College in Illinois. He was managing partner of Synergy Strategists, an education consulting group.

DONALD G. CRIST was at the right place at the right time in Illinois for the beginning of the community college movement. In the early 70's Don began teaching on a part-time basis at Carl Sandburg College. He left the public school for the community college in 1977, and for 30 years thereafter held positions of tenured faculty member, program director, division chairperson, dean, vice-president of instruction, and president. He was given a distinction of President Emeritus upon his retirement in 2002. Don served as consultant/evaluator/team leader for the North Central Association of Colleges and Schools for many years. He was president of the Illinois Community College Council of Presidents in 2000/2001; he was the recipient of the George E. Warren Outstanding Business Leader Award in 1994, and the Illinois Community College Trustees Association Certificate of Merit in 2002. The Crist Student Center was named in Don's honor in 2003 by the Carl Sandburg College Board of Trustees. Don was a guest columnist for the Galesburg Register Mail from 2000-2003. For the pasat several years since his retirement he has served as a team leader for the accreditation of mortuary science programs for the American Board of Funeral Service Education, and has consulted with cmmunity colleges and technical colleges throughout the nation.

CHARLES R. NOVAK is President Emeritus of Richland Community College in Decatur, Illinois where he served for thirteen years until his retirement in 2001. During his career he served twenty three years as a community college president and a number of other years as a continuing education officer, a chief financial officer and a chief academic officer. From 1997 until 2003, Novak served as the Statewide Chair of the Illinois Leadership and Core Values Initiative. The purpose of the Initiative was to engage Illinois' forty-eight community colleges in serious discussions about the leadership behaviors which support the consideration of values and ethics in the workplace. Although retired, Novak has returned to work on many an occasion to help the community colleges. He now has over twenty five years experience as a community college president after serving in several interim roles. In 2006 the Illinois Community College Trustees Association awarded him the Certificate of Merit for his service to the community colleges of Illinois.

CONTACT INFORMATION
FOR THE AUTHORS:

John Anderson
P.O. Box 3437
Carefree, AZ 85377
480.390.1613
john33anderson@gmail.com

Donald Crist   [winter]
4612 Flagship Drive, #302
Fort Myers, FL 33919

Donald Crist   [summer]
12325 Long Street
Overland Park, KS 66213
913.645.3763
dcrist1@kc.rr.com

Charles Novak
9111 Old State Route 14
Du Quoin, Il 62832
217. 433.6605
charlesnovak@mac.com

74

www.ingramcontent.com/pod-product-compliance
Lightning Source LLC
Chambersburg PA
CBHW030004050426
42451CB00006B/104